A CLOCKWORK ORANGE
KUBRICK'S PRACTICE EXAMINED

Tom Ingham

KAPLAN PUBLISHING
Cambridge England

A CLOCKWORK ORANGE
KUBRICK'S PRACTICE EXAMINED
Copyright © Tom Ingham 2002

All Rights Reserved

No part of this book may be reproduced in any form,
by photocopying or by any electronic or mechanical means,
Including information storage or retrieval systems,
without permission in writing from both the copyright
owner and the publisher of this book.

ISBN 0 9544307 0 0

First Published 2002 by
Kaplan Publishing
K

Printed in Great Britain for Kaplan Publishing - **K**

A CLOCKWORK ORANGE
KUBRICK'S PRACTICE EXAMINED

For Alison & Sheila
Naturally

Introduction

A Clockwork Orange is an extremely useful film for new practitioners and enthusiasts to study. Every element in it is worthy of examination and by doing so, we can learn how a film maker's art is developed and about the choices that are made in order to bring a film to the screen.

During this examination of the film, I shall be pointing out aspects of Stanley Kubrick's film making process and attempting to show that nothing that we see on the screen or hear on the soundtrack is accidental or left to chance. It is my contention that every scene has something to show us as film makers and viewers and that within each scene individual shots can also be analysed.

To do this it is vital that, when watching the film, we ask ourselves a number of questions. We should be constantly questioning what it is that we are seeing and hearing and asking what choices have been made in the construction of the film. We can examine the technical aspects and see how the decisions about their uses affect the messages that are being transmitted to us as an audience. I shall be talking about Kubrick's use of the camera, his choice of angles, lenses and movement and how these elements affect the way that we view the different scenes in which they are used.

One striking element is the number of times a shot that I call deep-space-perspective is used. This is where the composition of the shot is arranged in front of a space that recedes into the far distance. I shall be asking why Kubrick seems to have a particular passion for this type of composition and noting examples of its use in his other films.

The use of light and shade and particularly certain lighting techniques will be looked at.

It will be interesting and useful to look out for the occasions on which elements from one scene are repeated in another.

Along with this, we should watch for the use of mirrors, both physical and when talking about characters.

Even thirty years later, the strong political messages that the film contains still have a resonance and we need to examine both how they were received at the time and what relevance they have for us today.

The visual style of this film is very strong and can tell us a great deal about the characters and their environments. In particular, Kubrick's use of colour is noteworthy.

As far as editing is concerned, we shall again see that choices have constantly been made as to which type of shot to use in conjunction with others, how long to hold them on screen and how and when to cut to the following scene.

The final and possibly most important point on the visual side is Kubrick's method of getting us to identify and sympathise with the main character of Alex. We should keep an eye out for the occasions on which our sympathies are aroused and when we feel that we have become part of the action. When we have identified them, we should then ask how these effects are produced and why we have been asked to become involved in the film in these ways.

This brings me onto the important but often ignored aspect of film making, the sound. Alex's voice-over runs throughout the film and it is worth noting how it changes with the different moods of the film.

Music plays an important role in all of Stanley Kubrick's films and A Clockwork Orange is no exception. I shall make the point that if we listen to the various different pieces of music, how and where they are used, we should be able to decipher links to other scenes as well as being aware that they have been chosen to convey specific messages.

Finally, I have included references to some of the locations used in the making of the film. The choice and use of these tells us how Stanley Kubrick was very concerned about the 'look' of his film and that finding particular kinds of architecture can influence the overall atmosphere of a production. In specific cases, it is also interesting to see how these places have changed over the years.

For further details of the locations used in 'A Clockwork Orange', please visit www.kubricklocations.com.

© Tom Ingham 2002

A *Clockwork Orange* is a film about a young man, Alex, whose exploits we follow as he and his gang terrorise the world in which they live. The story is divided into three parts, as book the by Anthony Burgess is, on which the film is based, and these are shown on screen in equal lengths of time of approximately 45 minutes each. The first part shows Alex and his droogs (gang members) as they variously assault, rape and murder in a seemingly motiveless way. Secondly we see Alex in prison for these crimes and then receiving the notorious Ludovico Treatment that is meant to 'cure' him of his violent tendencies. Finally he is released back into the community and we follow his final journey and ambiguous rehabilitation.

Although rarely seen in the country of its making and setting, until Kubrick's death, *A Clockwork Orange* is perhaps his most famous film. It is unique in the canon of British Kubrick films in that it is the only one set entirely in England. Except for the latter part of Barry Lyndon, this was the only occasion on which Kubrick used the country of his residence as the setting for one of his films.

A Clockwork Orange was shot almost entirely on location and is a singular Stanley Kubrick film in that it is the only example of his work that was made in locations that were both geographically and temporally close to those used for the setting of the film itself. The action takes place almost entirely within the Greater London area with the odd excursion into the Home Counties for scenes at the beginning, middle and end of the film.

"There was me, that is Alex..."

The first scene that we see was shot in one of the few sets that were built. The Korova Milk Bar appears only twice in the entire film but plays a significant part in the motivation of the action. Initially it is shown in a single reverse tracking shot that slowly reveals first Alex, then his droogs and finally the Milkbar and its interior decor. This is a very clear example of Kubrick's use of a stylistic theme that appears throughout his work. I shall refer to it as deep-space perspective. This way of revealing the scene by moving the camera backwards is used for specific reasons. By starting with an extreme close-up of Alex's face and then moving away from him, Kubrick is showing us the main character and only then revealing the other elements. Other filmmakers may have been tempted to start with a more conventional long shot to establish the scene and then move forwards to the subject of the shot but Kubrick allows us to see more and more of the setting rather than less and less. By doing this he is bringing in elements such as the erotic sculptures and the first words of nadsat (a language that Anthony Burgess invented for his book) printed on the wall behind the gang and giving us time to consider them. He is also allowing for the possibility that the space is limitless in that if the camera had moved forward we would have known that the shot would end as soon as it reached one or other of the characters' faces. This way Kubrick is in control. He has told us who the main character is by starting on his face and then backs up this point by the way that Alex is the only member of the gang who stares directly at the camera and who has a sly smile on his face. We then infer that this character who we have seen take a drink of 'MilkPlus' is the same person who is talking to us in the voice-over that continues throughout the rest of the film. He salutes us with his drink, immediately asking us to identify with him.

The music used in this scene also covers the opening titles and is an electronic composition by Walter Carlos. It is futuristic piece that builds slowly and includes a phrase that we hear again in the opening title music of The Shining, this time composed by Wendy Carlos (Walter became Wendy between the making of these two films). The phrase occurs as Alex takes a drink and again as the camera swoops across the lake in the later film. Both films are about menace and both pieces of music set the tone of their respective films.

"One thing I could never stand..."

The chronology of the location action follows a geographical path that starts on Wandsworth Common. The drunken tramp lies with a bottle of whisky in his hand singing 'Molly Malone' in an underpass that crosses Trinity Road just north of Windmill Road. In the film we initially see the underpass in long shot with a blank wall at the end that leads to the stairs that take you to the western side of the common. The other end from which Alex and the droogs enter is a sloping, paved pathway with the eastern common in the background. Nowadays this entrance has been replaced with a similar set of stairs to the other end. Another change is that the rectangular lights that line the underpass have been removed and in their place are lights that fit into the corner where the roof and wall meet.

This is another example of the use of the deep-space perspective that I mentioned earlier. In order to avoid casting a shadow, the camera is offset slightly to the left but we are still looking into the space along its length.

The scene again starts with an extreme close-up shot, this time it is of a whisky bottle, which then zooms out to the long shot of the tramp lying against the 45 degree incline of the underpass wall. This is when we become aware of the presence of the gang. We see the long shadows of four figures enter the scene and envelop the entire length of the underpass including the legs and torso of the tramp as if he is being engulfed and smothered by them. On the back wall, the shadows reveal the individual heads of the four characters who we have just seen in the Milkbar. During this shot we hear the clicking of footsteps on the concrete pavement. The scene then cuts to a shot looking back along the underpass towards the gang whose shadows are now approaching us. The large and menacing shadows give us the feeling of being threatened. This impression is produced using a technique that Kubrick uses again later in the film. He back lights the scene and uses the ceiling of the underpass to mask the light source that still has to be low enough to create the extremely long shadows. Only a small portion of the light is shown and this allows us to believe that it is a street lamp in the park behind the characters even though it is clearly far too powerful to be such. Using a wide-angle lens gives depth to the shot as well as encompassing the underpass and characters.

Kubrick lets us hear the first few lines of the song that the tramp is singing before he brings in Alex's voice-over in which he tells us that he cannot stand to see this kind of behaviour from anyone 'whatever his age might be', and, 'but more especially when he was real old like this one was'. He also refers to the song as 'filthy', a word he also uses to describe the tramp. This narration reveals some of Alex's motivations but hides others. We infer that he feels justified in beating the tramp up because he is 'a filthy, dirty, old drunky', who sings the 'filthy songs of his fathers and going blurp, blurp in-between as it might be a filthy old orchestra in his stinking rotten guts'. If we consider Alex's own downfall later in the film we see that it comes as a direct result of his singing in the bathroom of the writer's house.

His statement about the age of the tramp also shows that he is no respecter of authority or longevity and even the tramp's second song about fighting for his country only seems to initiate the beating that he receives. These two facets of the narration point to some of the themes of the film; firstly Alex is exercising free will; secondly the idea that he has no real reason to do what he does, he just enjoys it; and thirdly he has an ambivalent attitude towards power. He will exercise his power over those that he perceives as weaker than him and will rebel against those forces that wish to control him, but is prepared to kow-tow to authority if he feels that there is some advantage to him.

On a couple of occasions we cut to an extreme close-up, profile shot of Alex's face as he leans on his stick that he has stuck into the tramp's stomach. They bracket the tramp's explanation of his statement that he doesn't want to live 'in a stinking world like this'. A statement in which he gives us our first clue that this is neither an isolated incident nor an unusual gang of youths. He says, 'it's a stinking world because there's no law and order any more', and after he's talked about 'men on the moon', he says 'there's not no attention paid to earthly law and order no more'. Alex's breath condenses in the cold night air as if he is breathing out demonic smoke.

"Let's get her boys"

When they have beaten up the tramp, Alex and his droogs encounter another gang who are in the process of raping a young girl. This scene takes place in what looks like a derelict theatre with ornate decorations and a large floor space spanned by an octagonal ceiling. An abandoned casino on Tagg's Island that is in the middle of the River Thames just south of Hampton Court Palace was used. The casino and hotel to which it was attached no longer exist as they were torn down shortly after the film was made. Tagg's Island is now home to a number of houseboats and nothing remains of the original buildings.

The scene starts with an extreme close-up shot of a baroque painting of a garden setting on the ceiling that slowly zooms out and tilts down to reveal a stage on which five young men are attacking a half-naked woman. Although this shot was filmed in a pre-existing location, the ceiling of which was not painted for the film, it may not be too fanciful to suggest that Kubrick responded to its presence and specifically included it in the scene. It suggests the biblical idea of the fall from grace and loss of innocence, in the Garden of Eden, the story from Genesis, which is shown by the way that the shot echoes the fall by tilting down. Both of these are themes of the film. On the other hand it could merely have been included to contrast starkly with the action that it eventually reveals. In either case it seems to me that it is there for a specific purpose and is shot in such a way as to fulfil this. It is certainly not the conventional way to start such a scene.

We see the men strip the young woman, push and pull her around and then eventually drag her onto a pile of old mattresses. If we were in any doubt as to their intentions, Alex's voice-over tells us that they are 'getting ready to perform a little of the old in-out, in-out.' Alex then remains silent and allows us to see what they are doing.

Up until the point that we see Alex and his droogs, the scene is composed of four shots, two long shots and two close-ups. The first long shot is the one already mentioned and is followed by the first close-up in which we see exactly what is going on with the men and young woman. The second long shot gives us a visual clue that the action is being watched as it is shot from the point of view of Alex and his gang. The point of view shot also puts us, the audience, in the position of spectator, a position we shall see repeated during other acts of violence in the film. Just before we see the watching gang, we cut back to the second close-up. This shot ends just before the rape is about to take place and we cut to Alex and his droogs as they reveal themselves from the shadows.

Whatever we think about the beating that we have just seen given to the tramp, we are left in no doubt whose side we are on in the fight that is about to commence. Billy Boy and his gang are dressed in a mixture of camouflage jackets, boots and nazi regalia including the Iron Cross whereas Alex's gang are clothed almost entirely in white with its connotations of purity. The fight that ensues is a result of Alex not only interrupting Billy Boy's fun but also a tirade of abuse in which Alex questions Billy Boy's manhood and personal hygiene. Billy Boy then utters his only words, 'Let's get her boys.' This is literally what they were planning to do to the young woman who by this time has escaped but it is also interesting that he should use the word 'her' towards Alex which in this case would appear to imply a physical weakness. Alex's outburst has shown an articulate if abusive use of language that demonstrates his intellectual capabilities. This attribute has routinely been derided and it is no surprise that in England anti-intellectualism should be used as an insult to question Alex's manhood. A further example can be seen later in the film when Dim suggests that Alex's headache could have been caused by, 'using the gulliver (head) too much like maybe', referring to his habit of thinking. Alex himself talks about this just before he throws Georgie and Dim into the lake when he says,

'As we walked along the flatblock marina I was calm on the outside but thinking all the time...but suddenly I vidied that thinking was for the gloopy ones and that the omni ones used like inspiration and what bog sends...and I vidied right at once what to do.'

The ensuing fight in the casino is choreographed to Rossini's 'The Thieving Magpie' and includes the breaking of chairs and windows as well as other recognisable cinematic stunts. The music fits the setting of a casino/dance hall but its choice may not be purely terpsichorean. Kubrick often chooses pieces of music or songs whose very titles or lyrics give us a clue to their meaning in the scene. Many examples exist and in this case Alex and his droogs could be said to have stolen the entertainment that Billy Boy and his gang had planned for themselves. Later in the film we see Alex's hoard of booty collected from previous criminal excursions which looks very much like that of the bird that takes shiny objects almost as an automatic response to their reflective qualities.

The film in which this aspect of Kubrick's musical art has been perfected is his final work, 'Eyes Wide Shut' in which each scene is narrated by the music that accompanies it. This scene ends when Alex's gang is triumphant and we hear the sirens of police cars approaching. The main floor of the casino on which the fight takes place is lit in the same way as the underpass in the previous scene. A strong, low light floods through the doors and spills over the bodies of the defeated Billy Boy and his droogs while Dim continues to beat one of them with a chain. We have not been fully introduced to Alex's droogs but here is the first indication that this character lives up to his name. Alex has to whistle three times to get his attention and explain that they must all leave. This is a lesson that Alex will have to repeat more forcefully later in the film.

"The Durango 95 purred away real horrorshow"

They then steal the Durango 95 and terrorise other road users on the dark country lanes. During this short scene, we notice a reverse tracking shot as the road behind the car is illuminated as it rapidly recedes away from us. We may initially pass over this shot as a fairly standard back projected speeding car shot. What I believe is noteworthy about it however is the illumination that is used at the rear of the car. It is unusual for the background to be so brightly lit in this type of shot as we are normally expected to concentrate our attention on the occupants of the car. If the simple answer as to why we need the illumination is that there is no other light to show us the roadway as it disappears, then the next question is how the effect was achieved. To my mind, there are two ways in which this shot could have been produced. A camera could have been pointed out of the back of a vehicle onto which some lights had been attached. This would have required the driver to proceed on the 'wrong' side of the road with the risk of causing an accident as Alex does in the final film. However, I believe that there is much simpler and safer way that this shot may have been gathered. The car may have been driven on the legal, i.e. left hand side of the road, with its headlights on full beam and the camera pointing forwards. The film could then have been reversed when it was back projected in order to give the impression of a speeding car deliberately breaking the Highway Code.

The second thing that we notice during the car drive is the look on Alex's face. He tends to look fairly manic throughout the film but this particular expression recurs vividly on three later occasions. Firstly when he listens to Beethoven's 9th symphony for the first time in his bedroom; then during the Ludovico Treatment; and finally at the very end of the film as he imagines himself having sex in front of a wedding group. It seems to express his almost trance like state of mind induced by the sheer enjoyment at the experience that he is going through. This clearly does not apply to his experience of the Ludovico Treatment but in this case it is a pointer to the extreme emotions and physical discomfort that he is feeling.

"What we were after now was the old surprise visit"

Alex and the droogs now arrive at the writer's house that is identified by a sign 'HOME.' This scene is where the gang attack the writer and rape his wife all to the tune 'Singin' in the Rain.' The scene is reprised later in the film when Alex seeks sanctuary at 'HOME' and gives himself away by a further rendition of the song. This is probably the most complex of all the scenes in the film in that it was filmed in two locations and used two sets. The exterior is that of a house near Oxford and the interior is a home outside the village of Radlett north west of London very close where the Kubricks lived at the time. The hallway to the house and the mirrored bathroom are, apart from the Korova Milkbar and the prison reception area, the only examples of non-location shooting in the film.

This scene, although one of the shortest, has been talked about as being one of the most objectionable in the film because it contains the rape of the writer's wife. It is clearly a disturbing event made more so by the fact that we do not actually see the conclusion of the assault.

At the beginning of the scene there is an initial link to the action in the derelict casino. Alex has to again whistle to get the rest of the gang's attention. What follows appears to be a well-rehearsed routine with each member of the gang carrying out their allotted role with minimal instruction although Alex does give Dim an extra whistle to get him to fulfil his function. On the face of it, this is merely to restrain the woman but initially at least it is to hold her in such a way as to force her see what is happening to her husband who is being violently kicked on the floor. Once she has had her face slapped, however, Dim turns around in order to enjoy the spectacle himself.

It is well known that Kubrick himself used a hand held camera to shoot much of this scene but it is also worth noting that these shots are combined with more traditional camera movements. After the exterior shot of the house, where we see the gang approaching, crab-like, we see the writer at his desk. This shot continues, after we hear the doorbell, by tracking sideways to reveal the living area of the open-plan house in which his wife is sitting. She is placed in an ultra modern piece of furniture, which seems to represent a woman's breast, out of which she gets to answer the doorbell.

The tune the doorbell plays is the opening of Beethoven's fifth symphony, an in-joke that we will get when we later realise that Alex has a passion for this composer's music. The end of this shot is yet another example of deep-space-perspective and the woman recedes into it. We then cut to one of the sets, the mirrored corridor, which, again, is framed in such way as to give us a feeling of withdrawing space. The handheld camerawork is repeated later in the film during the scene with the Cat lady and these two scenes are very similar to each other. A function of the handheld camerawork is to give us the impression that we are taking part in the action, a device used again, in subsequent episodes. Once Alex has taped up the woman's mouth, he proceeds to destroy the study. At first this is a fairly conventionally framed shot but to add a dramatic effect, Kubrick tracks the camera forward as Alex pulls the bookcase down. He then returns to the main business that is the terrorising of the couple. The red body suit of the woman is mutilated with a pair of scissors and before he runs them up one of the legs to remove it completely, Alex pulls the area covering each breast out and proceeds to cut a hole in it. The image is horrific and we are left to make up our own minds as to what he could do if he so wanted. The horror of what is happening is shown by the reaction on the writer's face as he witnesses, on our behalf, the rape. He is shot in extreme close-up, his mouth having been stuffed with a ball and taped up, and therefore can only express his revulsion by the movement of his eyes. These take on an even more manic state because of the distortion produced by the wide-angle lens used to film them. He is held down on the floor so that his head is on its side and this allows it to fit neatly into the aspect ratio or shape of the screen. In all the long shots of the assault, bar one, we see the writer from behind as Georgie is holding him on the floor. The one shot that does not follow this rule is the one when Alex tells him to, 'Vidi well little brother, vidi well.' It is clear from the previous shots that he is addressing the writer but he is now, also looking directly at us. We, the spectators are again involved in the action that has been and will be taking place in the rest of the film. The difference between the writer and us is that we can leave but he can't. The very last shot of the scene is a close-up, handheld shot of the woman as something is happening to her, the particulars of which, again we are left to imagine.

"Freude, schöner Götterfunken"

The action then returns to the Milkbar that opened the film and this results in the beginning of Alex's downfall after he severely punishes Dim for being 'A bastard with no manners...' An overlapping sound edit starts the scene as we hear the title music that accompanied the opening scene begin while the writer's wife is being raped. We then see the gang troop slowly into the Milkbar. Dim is then allowed to show us more of his character. He approaches, alone, one of the erotic sculptures that we saw in the earlier scene and starts talking to it. The sculpture, one of many that line the Milkbar, is in the shape of a naked woman with very big white hair who is kneeling and thrusting her large breasts and nipples forward. Her arms are pushed out behind her and her hands are tied with a chain. He refers to the sculpture as Lucy and explains that he and the gang have been, 'working hard too'. It becomes clear that the sculpture is a machine for dispensing the 'MilkPlus' that is sold in the Milkbar. Dim inserts some money into a slot on the base of the machine and then apologises to the sculpture as he reaches between her legs and pulls a phallic lever that points upwards. Milk then shoots out of one of the nipples into a glass. Given what we have just witnessed in the previous scene, Dim's sentimental attitude to a stylised plastic shape is all the more ironic. The way that he refers to their previous actions as 'work' is noteworthy as it is repeated in a later scene when

Alex's father wonders what work Alex does of an evening.

As the gang are all seated in a line, we see a group of 'sophistos', one of who sings an aria from Beethoven's 9th. Alex exhibits his fixed gaze as he listens to the singing and does not break it even when Dim blows a raspberry. Alex then smashes his cane across Dim's legs to punish him and raises his glass in tribute to the female singer. Her look of shock is reinforced by the argument that follows. Dim rebels and Alex accepts his challenge of a fight. At this point whatever little intellect Dim has, takes control and he thinks better of it. He recommends that they all go home for some 'spatchka' (sleep). The argument is shot in such a way so as to reinforce the words that are being spoken. It contains two cutaway shots, the first of which is of the group, containing the singer, who are now no longer laughing and joking but are clearly concerned. The second shot is of two bouncers who are themselves relaxing on a sofa. They don't seem overly concerned but appear to be keeping a watchful eye on the situation. This involvement of other characters makes us appreciate the gravity of the situation.

"Municipal Flatblock 18A, Linear North"
When the night's fun is over, Alex returns, alone, to his home on an apparently dilapidated housing estate. This and the scene the following day when Alex is challenged by his droogs was filmed on what was then a modern and newly built housing estate in southeast London. Thamesmead South was so new at the time that signs of construction can be seen in the background of some of the shots. The lake into which

Alex throws Dim and Georgie is very much the same as when the film was shot. Some of the things that have changed are that notices forbidding swimming, railings on some of the walkways and replacement windows have all appeared. The trees have grown but ironically the general state of repair is much closer now to that envisioned in the film than it was at the time. On a hot summer's day in 1999 a burnt out car stood in an empty car park and refuse was strewn about the place in a way that was very reminiscent of the establishing shot in the scene. Given the weather conditions and the time of year, it was surprising that the place was almost entirely deserted which seemed odd for what was supposedly designed as a leisure facility.

The scene starts with a tracking shot of Alex walking through an open area covered in discarded furniture and other debris. Two things that we hear are worth mentioning. Firstly the music that accompanies the rest of the scene is initiated by Alex whistling the first few notes. This pre-empts the revealing of his love of music and tells us that it is used for a specific purpose. He then tells us that he lives with his 'dadda and mum'. This childlike use of language is in stark contrast to what we have heard so far and is a precursor to the revealing of a piece of information that we may not be aware of yet. Alex is a child and although his age is not stated, we will soon learn that he is a schoolboy. This fact makes his previous and future actions all the more disturbing. The language is also sentimental and reveals a softer side to his nature. He also tells us where he lives. 'Municipal Flatblock 18A, Linear North' sounds faceless and impersonal and fits well with the Eastern European feel of the environment. The film was made during the middle of the Cold War and both the name and look of the setting correlates with our idea of Soviet Bloc housing at the time.

The walls in the lobby of the tower block are decorated with classical male figures on which graffiti has been scrawled. This takes the form of phallic symbols and also sexually suggestive phrases such as 'If it moves, kiss it' and 'Suck it and see'. The defacement of these images coupled with the vandalised lift add to the impression of dilapidation and degradation.

We then see him urinating in his bathroom. Many scenes in other films have been shot in toilets but we rarely see the act in as much detail. One reason for including this short scene apart from to reinforce the earthy side of Alex's character is to introduce us to the decor of his home. The bathroom walls are covered in alternating diamond shapes of yellow, silver and orange. We will see later that this is typical of the kind of decoration that appears in the rest of the flat but is in stark contrast to Alex's bedroom. This is first shown in the reflection of a large mirror onto which Alex puts his false eyelashes. Although it does contain elements such as the carpet and bedspread that are brightly coloured, the main motif of the room is white. It is more sophisticated than the rest of the flat and is reminiscent of the writer's house.

"It was gorgeousness and gorgeosity made flesh"

After removing some money from his pockets, we see him add it to his stash as mentioned earlier. He then opens another draw in which there is a large snake. We learn later that his name is Basil. Basil is placed on a branch sticking out of the wall and takes his place in the story. He is not there just to show Alex's love of animals that is sometimes seen as a trait attributed to despots and tyrants, but also for erotic purposes. Alex starts to play Beethoven's 9th on his clearly expensive music system and we see Basil sniffing a painting of a naked woman, although he is placed discreetly over her private parts. The image of the woman is similar to the figures that we have seen in the Milkbar but even more so to the pictures that we shall soon see on the walls of the Cat lady's room. She is holding her legs apart, smiling and Basil therefore appears to be performing a sexual act on her. When we come to the Cat lady scene we will note that Alex sees her paintings and appears to be shocked by them. A strange reaction since he has one of his own. The Cat lady lives alone and her decor implies a fascination with the female body. These points and the sexual nature of the paintings seem to provoke a prudish reaction in Alex to the connotations of lesbianism.

If a snake and nudity remind us, as the painting of the garden did in the casino scene, of the tale of Adam and Eve, then the biblical metaphors are emphasised by the four figures of Christ that are below the painting. They are filmed and the shots are edited together in such a way as to give the impression that they are dancing. The figures are standing in an unusual way in that they each have one foot forward and an arm raised. They wear the crown of thorns and the hands have nails through them. It could be considered, at the very least, blasphemous but it ties in neatly with what we see now and later in the form of Alex's pornographic visions.

"Such lovely pictures"

Following the dance routine we see Alex's stare of reverie that reminds us of the picture of Beethoven that we were shown at the beginning of the musical sequence. Both of their sets of eyes have a fixed gaze and the looks on their faces are inscrutable. Alex's gaze appears to imply that he is masturbating or at least enjoying his visions in a similar way. We cut back to Ludwig Van before entering Alex's head and seeing his 'such lovely pictures'. We see a sequence of shots starting with a bride in white being hanged. This is followed by Alex with blood dripping from his vampire teeth. This shot is placed in between all of the other shots. An explosion in the ground is followed by another explosion producing flames. The final two shots are of cavemen being crushed by falling rocks and another image of fire. All of these images involve death or destruction and some appear to be taken from other films. What I think is important is the recurring image of Alex. It is one of the few times that he stares directly at us, again involving us with his thoughts. The exaggerated make-up and teeth are fairly absurd and childish but no more so than the dancing Christs that we have just seen. Alex has no sense that any of this is offensive; he sees it all as comical. The image of a vampire is interesting in that it needs blood to survive and carries out its life at night. When we see Alex it is usually indoors or at night and when he is released from the Ludovico Centre, it is in daylight and he becomes vulnerable. He also loves blood. He doesn't drink it but he likes the sight of it and to make it flow.

"Bit of a pain in the gulliver mum"

The music continues as we learn that Alex is a schoolboy who has been playing truant when his mother tries to wake him. She is shot in the hallway of the flat and we again see the garish decor. Other examples are shown in the kitchen, which has the same colour scheme as the bathroom but this time arranged in squares, and the living room with its silver embossed walls and modern furniture. This colour scheme recurs at other points in the film. We see it in the wigs that some women and the erotic sculptures in the Milkbar wear along with their artificial pubic hair. It is very clear in the music shop, not only in the decor and clothing, but also in the ice-lollies that the girls are eating. Finally, the most striking example is the end credit sequence when the cast and crew's names are displayed over alternating brightly coloured backgrounds. The examples clash with the cooler shades of the writer's house and the more sombre environment of the prison and Ludovico Centre. The contrast seems to point up the different attitudes and situations that Alex finds himself in. When he is relaxed and behaving in a 'normal' teenage way, in the music shop, chatting up girls, at home with his parents, the colours reflect this ordinary view of domesticity and childhood activity. On the other hand, when he is either committing acts of violence or being punished for such, his clothes and the decor seem to reflect the cold, drab or harsh environment in which he finds himself.

We see that Alex has a combination lock on his bedroom door and as he leaves the room we again see Beethoven staring at us from the window blind. It could be seen as a metaphor in that Alex is using him to keep

out the bleak outside world, an instance of which we
see through the kitchen window when his parents are
discussing his nocturnal activities. As Alex wanders
around the flat in his underpants, he passes an open
door through which we catch the merest glimpse of
someone sitting on a bed. This turns out to be Mr
Deltoid, Alex's 'post-corrective advisor'. The scene
that follows involves Alex denying any wrongdoing and
Mr Deltoid knowingly warning him of what the future
holds if he carries on breaking the law. We assume,
from the decor and the brightly coloured wigs that we
see in front of the window, one of which we have just
seen his mother wearing, that this is Alex's parent's
room.

"A big black mark I tell you for every one we don't reclaim"

The dialogue gives us a lot of information about
Alex's past but also points to one of the ways that
violence is dealt with in the film. Mr Deltoid tells Alex
and us that Billy Boy and his gang have been taken to
hospital. This is an example of the fact that apart from
the writer being confined to a wheelchair and the cut
to Dim's hand, none of the consequences of Alex's
violence are shown on screen. They are all reported.
The tramp tells his friends that he was beaten up by
Alex, the writer tells us that his wife has died, Mr
Deltoid informs Alex that the Cat lady is dead.
However, this pattern is not repeated when the
violence happens to Alex. In the bedroom scene Mr
Deltoid brings his hand violently down on Alex's
genitals. Dim smashes a bottle of milk in Alex's face and
we see the blood and bandage later in the police

interrogation room where he is beaten up again, the consequences of which we see when Mr Deltoid enters and spits in his face. We witness his pain during the Ludovico Treatment and also when he is beaten and humiliated in front of the dignitaries. Once released, he is first set upon by the tramps and then beaten up and left for dead by his former friends. Finally he throws himself out of a window to escape the torture of listening to Beethoven's 9th and we then see him in hospital. In this way Kubrick is asking us to identify with his suffering, however much we are revolted by his own violence.

Mr Deltoid asks whether there is a devil that gets into Alex. From the recent 'lovely pictures' that we have seen, it seems clear that there is something demonic about his interior world.

The music encroaches into the beginning of the scene and fades away just before Alex speaks. Once Mr Deltoid has assaulted Alex's private parts, he is left alone on the bed and the rest of the shot contains him alone. The comic ending of this scene has caused some people a problem. Mr Deltoid takes a drink from a glass that has a set of false teeth in it. He holds the glass in his hand and we see what it contains. He is unaware of this as he is talking to Alex. The few seconds that follow are full of anticipation as we wait to see if will take another drink. He does and then realises what we have known for a while and tries to wipe his mouth to get rid of the taste. It is, in one sense, a piece of throwaway humour and could be criticised for undermining the serious words that have just been spoken. On the other hand, Mr Deltoid is clearly a comic character with his affected use of language and grinning face and we are in no doubt that Alex sees him as such. This view is not going to be altered by his warnings of dire consequences or 'the stripy hole' (prison).

"You are invited"

We then see Alex indulging in two of his favourite pastimes, sex and music. He takes two young girls home and they romp around the bedroom to the accompaniment of classical music. The scene in which he meets the two girls is set in a music shop but was filmed in the Chelsea Drugstore on the Kings Road. This is now an outlet of McDonalds.

The scene in the music shop starts with a shot of one of the girls looking at an illuminated music chart. Alex then walks into view. The camera tracks backwards as he looks around the shop in a relaxed manner. He is wearing a purple Edwardian style coat but still carries his cane. This outfit is in stark contrast to his droog uniform. He ends up at a counter on which is displayed the soundtrack to 2001, Kubrick's previous film. He then chats up the two girls who are licking phallic shaped ice-lollies. He invites them to come and 'hear angel trumpets and devil trombones.' He also derides their choice of music and refers to it as 'fuzzy warbles.' One of the groups that we hear mentioned by one of the girls is 'Goggly Golgol'. Alex may dismiss such music but we see that he also listens to it as in order to play his Beethoven the previous night, he has had to first remove a tape by this group. He takes the girls home and has sex with both of them. The scene is set to Rossini's William Tell Overture. The music starts in the usual way with the trumpet fanfare but as Alex and the girls enter the bedroom, it changes to a speeded up, electronic version. This fits with the action of the sex scene that is also shown in fast-motion. The music starts at a medium pace, speeds up, reaches a climax and then trails off. A bit like sex really.

"He are here, he have arrived"

We then come to the scene in which Alex's supremacy is challenged by his droogs. He encounters them in the stairwell of the block of flats. It is interesting to note the way in which he greets them. He asks them 'to what do I owe the extreme pleasure of this surprising visit?' He is being ironic as he is clearly far from pleased to see them but another indicator is his use of the words 'surprising visit'. This is very close to the way that he described the gang's invasion of the writer's house. He now feels vulnerable in a similar, if far less violent, way to his victims of the previous night. The music from the previous action overlaps the start of the scene as Alex saunters down the stairs. The first thing that we notice is Dim pretending to drive a car in the same way that Alex was doing in the dark country lanes. It is clear that Alex is uncomfortable at having his droogs visit him at home as it puts him at a disadvantage. At this point Georgie utters his first words. His sinister tone heralds the 'new way' that the gang have been plotting. He complains that they are not carrying out big enough crimes to satisfy their needs. When Alex says that if they need anything they just take it, Georgie accuses him of thinking and talking, 'sometimes like a little child', and that they will, 'tonight pull a man sized crast'. Alex goes along with this but the droogs insist on some MilkPlus first. Throughout the scene, Dim is sitting in a pram, one of the wheels of which he has been using as a steering wheel in his pretend car. This reinforces our view of Dim as a childlike character.

"For now it was lovely music that came to my aid"
The following scene is shot entirely in slow motion. Alex and the droogs walk beside the lake and Alex exacts his violent revenge for their conspiracy against him. The characters walk towards us in deep space perspective and as the shot is filmed with a telephoto lens, the background is foreshortened. The violence is accompanied by part of The Thieving Magpie and involves Alex throwing Georgie and Dim into the lake. He pretends to help Dim out but cuts the back of his hand with a knife. The only character not involved is Pete who backs away. Pete is a peripheral character who merely mutters and is literally on the edge of the group whenever we see him. He only appears briefly in the next two scenes and then is never seen again.

"We're not little children"
When the gang have recovered from their swim in the lake, they retire to 'The Duke of New York' pub where Alex says that everything is back the way it should be. The name of the pub shows the link between the old and the new. New York, a modern, vibrant metropolis, is combined with the traditional name of many English public houses.

Even though Alex appears to have literally beaten the droogs into submission at the lake, they have been scheming behind his back and he takes little persuading that there are easy pickings at a house in the country inhabited by a lone woman and her cats. He tells us that, 'now they knew who was master and leader - sheep thought I'. We will hear and see sheep referred to in a later prison scene but we are about to be shown that Alex has underestimated his droogs. This is where Alex commits the crime for which he is convicted. Shenley Lodge is where he encounters and kills the Cat lady.

"What the bloody hell do you think you're doing?"

We initially see the Cat lady as she exercises on the floor of a large room decorated with highly sexual paintings. She is also surrounded by cats, animals that are traditionally seen as promiscuous. Kubrick uses a wide-angle lens for this and other shots in the scene. This creates not only the illusion of a greater space but also a slightly unreal perspective, the disorientating effect of which is added to by the use of a hand held camera. Kubrick uses this later in the scene in the same way as he did earlier in the writer's house. The Cat lady is not taken in by Alex's pleas for help so he has to resort to another method of entry. The gang go to the back of the house and the way that they move is very similar to the crab like walk that they used to approach the writer's house.

Once inside, Alex suddenly appears in the room with the Cat lady just has she has finished a telephone conversation with the police. Her accent and way of talking reveal her to be of a higher class than Alex and she later refers to herself and his other victims as, 'real people'. She also calls Alex a, 'wretched, slummy bedbug' and apart from Alex himself at the end of the film, is the only character that swears.

As mentioned before, Alex appears to be offended by the paintings on the walls and especially by a sculpture in the form of an enormous phallus. When he plays with and hits the sculpture, producing a comic up and down motion, the Cat lady becomes incensed and starts to attack him. Her weapon of choice is ironically a bust of Beethoven. Alex defends himself and eventually attacks the Cat lady with the phallus and it therefore becomes a symbol of violence as well as of sex.

At this point the camerawork changes from conventional to hand held. As mentioned before, this is one of many similarities to the rape scene in the writer's house and is a visual link to that previous crime. Another link is again the music. Although the earlier scene was accompanied by Alex's singing, what led up to it was 'The Thieving Magpie', music that supplements this action. The full horror of the violence is, once again, left to our imagination, as the final image of the fight is a painting depicting the open mouth of a woman. For added emphasis the Cat lady's scream is mixed with the squealing of a cat. The scene is all the more powerful for this as it is unnecessary to see the crushed skull of the woman for us to understand and imagine what is going on.

(Again, this is not squeamishness on Kubrick's part as we are about to graphically see when Alex becomes a victim of a head injury.)

The extremely short sequence at the end of the scene is in fact made up of a series of close-up shots of parts of the paintings. There is the mouth, a breast hanging on a washing line with a male hand close by, a pair of breasts and female genitalia, all presented subliminally for no more than a few frames at a time. A very strong link is made here between sex and violence.

Yet another link to a previous scene is heard as he stands over his victim. A lull in the music allows us to hear a police siren in the same way as one appeared at the end of the Billy Boy scene. This time, however, Alex does not need to whistle to get anyone's attention. He seems to understand what he has done and desperately fumbles with the locked door. Once outside, he expects to escape with his gang but they attack him and leave him for the police to find and arrest.

"I won't say a single solitary slovo..."

We next see Alex in an interrogation room. The room is a blank square space with a single naked light bulb hanging from the ceiling. This scene was shot in a back room of Brunel University in Uxbridge.

Although we don't see his face immediately, we are instantly aware that Alex is in a relaxed mood. This is shown by a shot of a police officer resting his head in his hand and by Alex's hand hanging from his braces. The police officer is tired and when Alex says that they are wasting their time and that he isn't going to say anything, we assume that we have come in at the end of a lengthy interrogation. At this point he is standing and the first part of the scene is shot using conventional camera work with close up shots to introduce the characters. We can just hear, in the background, the sounds of typing and whistling which reinforce the idea that we are in a police station. After Alex has said that he understands the law, the senior police officer, tells another detective to, 'show our friend Alex here that we know the law too, but that knowing the law isn't everything'. What follows is an example of police brutality.

We now know that Alex is outnumbered three to one but even though he clearly feels threatened, he continues to be provocative. He belches in the face of one of the officers and when the officer reacts by pressing on Alex's facial wound, Alex grabs his testicles. The first officer then jumps up and hits Alex in the face to get him to stop. The action then cuts to the exterior of the interrogation room. What is interesting about this is that we do not see the full beating that Alex receives but we will see the effects of it when we re-enter the room. This is in contrast to the examples of his victims where we see the act but not the consequences. The short sequence outside the interrogation room serves to reintroduce Mr Deltoid. It also confirms that this is a police station as there is another officer in uniform sitting at a desk. The conversation between this officer, Mr Deltoid and the officer who emerges from the interrogation room is matter of fact and has the purpose of telling us that this is an unfortunate but routine situation.

"He must be a great disappointment to you sir"

When we re-enter the interrogation room, the first thing that we notice is that this part of the scene is shot using a wide angle lens and that the shots of the police officers are now from Alex's point of view. We are being asked to see the situation from his viewpoint and also to realise that he is now experiencing the disorientation that his victims have endured. This is reinforced by the fact that the first shot is from a very low angle and as the senior enters the room he throws some paper towels at the camera. We then cut to Alex who is now lying on the floor with blood on his face and on the wall beside him. The paper towels are now on the floor next to him. The rest of the scene consists of cuts between this point of view shot, which includes all of the police officers and Mr Deltoid standing over Alex and various shots of Alex lying on the floor. These other shots are not from the exact point of view of the other men, as Alex does not look directly in the camera. He looks slightly to the side and when Mr Deltoid crouches down, we see the top of his head. The use of different types of shot indicates the role of identification in the latter part of this scene. We see exactly what Alex sees and therefore experience the scene as he does. He is overpowered by the other men and is vulnerable to their attacks. We feel the menace in the same way that Alex's victim, the writer felt when he was forced to, 'vidi well'. Mr Deltoid reacts to Alex's assertion that they are torturing him by saying that he hopes, 'to god that it will torture you to madness'. As we shall see, it is not the fact that he has killed that will have this effect but the very treatment designed to stop him repeating his acts of violence. When offered the chance to give Alex, 'a bash in the chops', Mr Deltoid prefers to spit in his face, in some ways, a more violent option. Alex calmly wipes the spittle from his mouth, looks at it, smiles and throws the towel away defiantly.

"This is the real weepy and like tragic part of the story..."

The next part of the film is set in a prison. We first see it from the air as the camera circles the building in three shots that get closer and closer to the compound. These shots were taken over Wandsworth Prison. The prison reception area where Alex is examined was a set built in a factory near Borehamwood. The rest of the interiors of the prison, including the cell blocks and yards, were filmed at Woolwich Barracks.

As Alex enters the prison, he is dressed in what we assume is his suit for appearing in court. It certainly looks very different to anything that he has worn so far. He is shouted at by the chief guard and goes through the induction process. He is given number and told to strip after he has handed over all of his property. The scene starts with Alex telling us that, 'this is the real weepy and like tragic part of the story beginning oh my brothers and only friends'. Further identification with Alex is asked for here. He is appealing to us to sympathise with his plight. Later in the same voice-over he refers to himself as, 'your friend and humble narrator'. This is the beginning of Alex's change in the use of language. We will see a further example when he talks to the chaplain. We don't believe for one minute that he has changed but we know that he is trying to convince the people around him that he has. The initial spur for this is that he has been imprisoned for fourteen years with, 'smelly perverts and hardened prestutniks'. Later we see that this change in attitude is a way of trying to get out of prison. As he stands outside the reception area he continues to talk, but this time about his parents and how he has let them down. This is the only occasion that he appears to consider their feelings at all.

The whole action takes place 'by the numbers' and Alex soon learns that this is the only acceptable way. He is outnumbered again and although he smiles when he says that he has been convicted of murder, he is quickly answering the chief officer clearly and precisely. The reception area is again shot with a wide-angle lens and makes use of deep-space-perspective. The walls are lined on two sides by identical cardboard boxes, stacked floor to ceiling. Until his transfer to the Ludovico Centre, he is referred to by his number, 655321, and his clothes that would identify him as an individual are stored in one of these boxes. He has become a number on a list. The boxes are like little coffins in which the prisoners' identities are literally mothballed until their release. As Alex strips, he is asked what we assume is a standard series of questions that all convicted prisoners must answer. After each answer another officer states, aloud, the item of clothing that has just been removed. This series of questions, answers and statements is choreographed in such a way that none of the dancers ever overlaps or get in each other's way. Throughout this question and answer session we are shown a clear example of Alex's duplicity. He answers the questions in the way that is required but we can see and hear that he is only taking the process as seriously as he has to. He makes four mistakes during his induction. He fails to call the chief 'Sir'. He literally steps over line. He throws his bar of chocolate onto the desk. He finally refers to his religion as C of E rather than the Church of England. We have already seen Alex's disdain of religion in his bedroom and here is another very mild example. In the next two scenes we will see that although we know that he still holds these attitudes, he will modify his outward behaviour to fit in with his surroundings.

On one of the pillars, behind the chief officer, in the reception area, there hangs a collection of white braces, very similar to those that we have recently seen Alex wearing. They stand out like the trophies of a hunter and are similar to the pelts of wild animals or scalps. In this way we are being shown that Alex is now trapped and will become just another set of braces on the wall.

The final question in this series coincides neatly with the removal of Alex's underpants and is, 'are you now or have you ever been a homosexual?' The chief officer then proceeds to conduct an internal examination with the use of a torch clenched between his teeth. There is an element of comedy here as the question and answer session continues as if nothing out of the ordinary is happening. It is also interesting to note that the chief officer's gaze is initially directed towards Alex's genitals. The sexuality of many of the characters is ambivalent and we will see in the following scenes that this is a recurring theme.

"What's it going to be then, eh?"

The next scene starts with a close up shot of a chaplain. He asks the question, 'What's it going to be, eh?' These are almost the exact words that Alex uses at the beginning of each of the three sections of the book on which the film is based. In the book, the chaplain also uses this phrase and it is interesting that he is talking about choosing between right and wrong whereas Alex is asking firstly what act of violence he should carry out, then what is going to happen to him in prison and finally what he should do with his life now that he has been 'cured'. In the first section he has free will. In prison he can choose between towing the line and giving himself up to prison life. Finally, his choice of action has been taken away from him and he can see only one way out.

During this scene Alex is sitting next to the chaplain but we are initially unaware of this. What we first see is the chief officer standing by a window looking straight ahead. He is shot from a low angle, to reinforce our view of him as a powerful figure, and his attention is eventually caught by something below him. A look of disgust comes over his face and he purses his lips. We then discover the reason for his distaste. An older prisoner is also pursing his lips towards Alex and this is when we see that he is separate from the others. He sits impassively staring back with his arms folded. We cut back to the other prisoner who continues looking at Alex and then winks. What follows is a close up of the chief officer as he surveys the scene but eventually turns away. Later in the scene Alex tells us that he has been in prison for two years and that he has met, 'leering criminals and perverts ready to dribble all over a luscious young malchick like your storyteller'. The chief officer's reaction implies that he doesn't like what is going on but has no power to stop it and that Alex could not turn to him or any of the other officers for help. Alex also tells us that they have beaten him up so his only alternative seems to be religion and the protection of the chaplain.

Two other elements of the scene are also worth mentioning. Firstly that the chaplain's sermon is interrupted twice. We first hear a belch like the one that Alex used in the police station. This makes the chaplain tell of even more lurid fates that will befall unrepentant sinners. This speech is further undermined by a farting noise at which point he gives up and makes them sing a hymn. This sound is reminiscent of the one that Dim used to punctuate the singing of the aria in the Milkbar.

The other element to note is the hymn itself. Alex talks over most of it but we do hear the first few lines and we can see the words projected behind him.

> 'I was a wayward sheep
> I did not love the fold
> I did not love my shepherd's voice
> I would not be controlled
>
> I was a wayward child
> I did not love my home
> I did not love my father's voice
> I ....

Not only could these words be taken as a literal narration of Alex's story so far but also it is useful to note the use of the word 'sheep'. Alex referred to his droogs as sheep just before they betrayed him to the police and in the Christian religion Christ is a shepherd. A shepherd is needed to keep his flock safe from predators and Alex, as we will see is certainly a 'wolf in sheep's clothing'. He is a dangerous young man who has wrapped himself in the cloak of religion in order to gain the trust of the chaplain and to further his desire for freedom.

"Father, I have tried have I not?"

He shows the duplicitous nature of his character in the next scene. We see the chaplain walking around the room and notice that Alex is sitting at one of the tables reading a large bible. He smiles at Alex and walks off. Alex smiles back and mouths some words to himself as if he is reading a passage silently. While he is smiling at the chaplain he tells us what he really thinks of him. He calls him a, 'bolshy great burly bastard'. When he also tells us that the chaplain has taken a shine to him we know that Alex will try to use this to his advantage. The chaplain likes him because he has become, 'very interested in the big book'. Alex then shows why he has become interested in the Bible. We are again treated to one of his visions. This time, however it is made up of three longer scenes in which Alex takes centre stage. The sequence starts as Alex stares off into the distance. The first scene begins with a shot of a Christ figure dragging a cross. We see that he is being lashed as he walks along. Eventually it is Alex that is revealed to be the person doing the lashing and he is dressed as a Roman soldier. We then cut back to Alex and he now closes his eyes. The second scene is of Alex fighting and cutting the throat of an enemy. He is no longer a Roman but what he calls a 'yehudy'. Finally we cut to a shot of Alex on his back as someone feeds him grapes. The shot zooms out to reveal him lying on a bed surrounded by three semi-naked women. Our expectations here are again undermined. We might expect a young man,

39

imprisoned for fourteen years in a brutal environment to see himself as a victim. His reading of the bible may also bolster this view and this could engender feelings of identification with the misery described therein. His utter confidence in his own flawless character leads him to see himself in the roles of crucifier, conqueror and hedonist. Over the first scene he says that he, 'could vidi (himself) helping in and even taking charge of the tolchoking and the nailing in'. During the second and third scenes he says that he, 'didn't so much like the latter part of the book which is more like all preachy talking than fighting and the old in out'. He clearly prefers the Old to the New Testament. If we needed proof that Alex still retains his blood lust he has just given it to us.

The chaplain awakens him from his reverie as he places a hand on his shoulder. It is almost as if he has noticed Alex's trance-like state and has decided to distract him from it. We learn from Alex that he has been a good boy and the chaplain confirms that he has, 'shown a genuine desire to reform'. Alex then wants to ask him a question in private and they walk off together towards the bookshelves. The chaplain puts his hand on Alex's shoulder and the camera tracks backwards as they walk towards us. Alex's hands are folded in front of him and his head is bowed. Both figures are framed in yet another example of deep-space-perspective. The chaplain assumes that he wants to talk about the sexual desires that prisoners inevitably feel but Alex merely stops walking, turns to the chaplain and tells him that he wants to know about the Ludovico Treatment. The chaplain clearly has strong reservations and says that not only has it not been proven to work but that there may also be adverse side effects. In response to Alex's questioning, the chaplain takes his hand off his shoulder and looks him straight in the eye. He goes on to state his reservation that the treatment may not truly make someone good and that, 'when a man cannot choose, he ceases to be a man'. We will hear him repeat this very point when Alex has been 'cured'. Throughout this conversation, Alex exhibits two of his new character traits. We have already seen his false piety but he now also pretends to be ignorant and unable to understand the concepts that the chaplain is talking about. We know from what we have seen and heard before that this must be a calculated act designed to manipulate the chaplain. The chaplain puts his hand back on Alex's shoulder and they pray together.

"You're absolutely right sir"

In the exercise yard we see the prisoners walking around a circle painted on the ground. As this is a confined area, Kubrick uses a wide-angle lens that, again, not only gives the impression of space but also turns the square yard into an example of deep-space-perspective. We will see shortly that this is used for dramatic effect. The next shot is along the corridor of cells at the end of which we see and hear a group of figures. The chief officer barks his orders and a gate is opened. The figures approach and we can distinguish one in particular. Not only is he at the front of the group but he is also wearing a lighter coloured, better quality suit than the rest of them. There are two other members of the group also wearing suits as well as the chaplain. One of these turns out to be the governor and the other is probably the minister's assistant or deputy. His suit is not as light as the minister's but is lighter than the governor's which is very close in shade to the prison officers' and prisoners'. We hear Elgar's 'Pomp and Circumstance' and these elements combine to give the impression that the first man is of great importance. This is reinforced by him entering an empty cell unaccompanied, something we assume he could not do if he was not a powerful figure. He turns out to be The Minister of the Interior. Two armed guards, thus emphasising the minister's stature, accompany the whole group. When he enters the cell, he inspects the room and its contents. It is, of course, Alex's cell and this is shown by what he finds there. The first thing he notices is a bust of Beethoven, white this time. He picks it up but does not seem to be too impressed as he then notices the more predictable nude photographs on the wall. He looks around the room and as he is about to leave he sees a picture in a frame. This is Ludwig Van again and he picks the picture up. He looks back to the bust, scans the room again and walks out. He was expecting to see the nude pictures but was surprised by other objects. As the cell has two beds, we assume that the nude pictures belong to the other prisoner. This short scene plays no part in the motivation of the following action, as the minister has no idea when he meets Alex that he has just visited his cell. The function of the scene is to remind us of Alex's tastes and appetites and so to reinforce their significance in later scenes.

Before the minister emerges into the exercise yard, the chief officer stands to attention and orders the prisoners to line up for inspection. He then salutes and the group come outside. The militaristic overtones of these actions support the idea that we are seeing a future penal system based on an idea of how society might change and accept martial laws. Alex refers to the forces of law and order as 'milicents' earlier in the film, this word having clear associations with the 'military'.

We then cut to a shot along the line of prisoners. As this is filmed with a wide-angle lens, and as Alex is in the foreground, the whole shot has the disorientating effect that we have seen before. As the group walk towards us, the minister and governor discuss penal conditions and reform. All of the prisoners, including Alex, remain motionless as the minister hints at the new 'treatment' that will 'cure' these criminals.

As he walks past Alex and says that 'punishment means nothing to them, you can see that, they enjoy their so called punishment', Alex reacts and says, 'you're absolutely right sir'. This shows his quick thinking and that he is prepared to take risks. He knows that he should remain silent but sees the opportunity to advance himself. We know from previous scenes that prison has made him expert at this.

The minister's reaction takes us by surprise. We expect him to be as angry as the chief guard that a prisoner has dared to speak in his presence. On the contrary, he seems delighted and smiles when he is told that Alex is a murderer. Alex himself still insists that it was an accident but this is no less than we would expect from him. It is interesting that it is the minister who instantly recognises Alex for what he is. He describes him as, 'enterprising, aggressive, outgoing, young, bold, vicious'. All this after having only seen him for a few seconds. Alex is selected for the treatment and the minister tells the governor that he is, 'perfect' and that, 'this vicious young hoodlum will be transformed out of all recognition'. We shall see soon enough that this prediction is an accurate one. He finally shows that he appreciates Alex for what he is by calling him, 'my boy' before he leaves.

"Shut your filthy hole you scum"

In the final scene in the prison we see Alex marched into the governor's office in order to sign forms for his transfer to the Ludovico Centre. By this time he knows what white lines are for and obediently stands to attention behind the one marked on the carpet. The office is old and shabby in contrast to the clothes and demeanour of the minister. The governor is a plain speaker and explains that he disapproves of the, 'new ridiculous ideas'. The book that lies on his desk again shows the differences between him and the minister. It is a copy of Wisden's Almanac and links him with traditional values and ideas. As he continues his biblical views on crime and punishment, Alex tries to interject. As he does so, the chief officer tells him to, 'shut your filthy hole, you scum'. He doesn't believe that Alex has changed and sides with the governor. He further asserts his authority when he orders Alex to answer the governor's question and later when he tells him to just sign the form in front of him and not to read it. Throughout this and all of the scenes in the prison, we are never presented with shots from Alex's point of view. This is very different from the scene in the police station in which these shots were used to imply Alex's subjugation. It seems that Alex has managed to stay in control despite the restrictions applied to him. He smiles as he signs the forms and grins as he throws the pen down when he has finished. The chief officer displays the same look of disgust as he did in the chapel and purses his lips in the same way.

"You'll have to watch this one"

The exterior of the Ludovico Centre is appropriately brutal and overpowering. The prison officers escort Alex across a concrete courtyard overhung by a menacing building that juts into the sky. This is another example of Stanley Kubrick's use of contemporaneous buildings that, at the time, looked futuristic and still hold some of that visual quality today. This is one way in which this location contrasts with the prison. Again, signs of the ongoing construction of the site can be seen in the background of the initial tracking shot. The scene was shot at the newly built Brunel University in Uxbridge in the far West of London close to where the now M4 and M25 meet. Nothing much has changed of the exteriors apart from some security grilles on some of the windows. The reception area in the film, shot in the entrance to the university's maths department is an open space with the exterior wall being made up of floor to ceiling glass panels. This remains the same today as do the cylindrical lights on the ceiling. What has changed is that fire doors and seating have been added. Brunel was used for the entire Ludovico sequence and also for the scene in which Alex is interrogated by the police after killing the Cat lady.

As Alex is led across the courtyard we hear another rendition of 'Pomp and Circumstance' that continues throughout the scene. The link here is to the minister.

The treatment that Alex is about to undergo is what the minister is relying on to solve the problem of violent crime and the music reminds us of this.

The chief officer again carries out his duties with military precision and this seems all the more ridiculous in the clean and bright surroundings that he is now in. His shouting of orders is out of place and is very different to the quiet and calm tone of the doctor. The doctor appears impatient with him and assures him that they will be able handle Alex. He is the first and last person to refer to Alex as a young man rather than a boy. Even the guard at the centre, although he is dressed in a similar way, is of a different breed. Not only is he referred to by his first name but he also asks Alex to, 'come this way please'. Before he releases him into the custody of the centre, the chief officer gives us one last reminder that Alex's behaviour is a sham. He says that he has been, 'a right brutal bastard...and will be again despite of all his sucking up to the prison chaplain and reading the Bible'. This neatly ties up the prison sequence and condenses it in our memory.

"We're going to be friends then aren't we Alex?"

We cut to the exterior of Alex's room where the guard is waiting. A doctor and nurse approach and the guard lets them into the room. They both wear medical uniforms and the whole scene introduces and reinforces the idea that Alex is here for treatment. The nurse prepares an injection of serum 114 (CRM 114 is the code machine in Dr Strangelove). Alex refers to the doctor as 'missus' throughout the interview. He uses this form of address to the female conspirator at the end of the film but calls the Cat lady 'Madam'. He is showing what he considers to be respect in the first two cases but is being merely sarcastic in the case of the Cat lady. In her case, he is in the position of power whereas he is a subordinate figure to the other two women. The doctor in this scene is stern and says, 'we're going to be friends then aren't we Alex?', in a rhetorical form, implying that he is going to behave himself. He asks whether the injection is to send him to sleep and she says, 'nothing of the sort'. We shall see that the idea is that he will literally be 'wide awake' during his treatment. Alex is very calm throughout this scene and has no idea of the horror that awaits him. We are as ignorant as he is, at this stage, but the doctor's demeanour gives a strong hint that he is not going to enjoy himself.

"Where I was taken to brothers was like no sinny I ever vidied before"

Enjoy himself he does not. Most of what he sees on the cinema screen is hidden from our view and we are subjected to the horrific vision of Alex restrained and forced to watch the films. He can't turn away in the same way that the writer was made to watch the rape of his wife. We at least have the option of closing our eyes or averting our gaze. We can almost feel the metal clamps on our own eyelids and the drip of the eye drops as they overflow and run down our cheeks. He doesn't mind too much at first and forgets his predicament by appreciating the images in front of him. He likes the scene in which a gang, dressed like his own, beat a man to a pulp. He says a very interesting thing during this sequence. He refers to, 'the red, red vino (blood)' and says, 'it's funny how the colours of the real world only seem really real when you vidi them on a screen'. We are, of course, watching a film and Kubrick uses an almost exact transposition from the book to draw our attention to the fact that however much we abhor what we are seeing and have seen, we are still watching. Many people enjoy the spectacle of violence, as is evidenced by Hollywood action movies, without appreciating the consequences of the real thing. In most cases, the violence that we see is sanitised and clean. In this case there is a layer of distance between the violence and us in that we know that we are watching a fiction but we are asked to believe that within that fiction, what Alex is forced to watch is real. The implication is that the man is really being beaten up and that the woman in the next episode is genuinely being gang raped.

"You're getting better"

During the next scene in which the female doctor explains to Alex how the treatment works, she is shot from below thus giving us a view of her as a powerful figure. Alex is unrestrained and there is no guard in the room but he is sensible enough to not try anything. He sees her as a genuine figure of authority and his only intention is to put up with the treatment and to get out of there.

"It's a sin"

In his next session of treatment, Alex is shown another set of films. We only see a small portion of them but what we are shown is supposed to imply something much worse. The films are of nazi soldiers in the Second World War. They march, bomb and destroy but we do not see any victims of these actions. No bodies or scenes from the camps are shown but in the context of the treatment, we are asked to imagine these pictures. They are just the sort of thing that Alex would have created in his mind's eye before but this time they are hidden from our view. We have seen them many times before and therefore they have all the more impact for being in our heads rather than on the screen. Many reviews of this film have talked about scenes in which Alex and his gang rape and kill even though it could be said that the final act is not actually presented on screen. The impression of the violence is so strong that we believe that we have seen something that is only in our imagination. In this case we infer the horror that Alex is witnessing and fully understand his physical distress that is induced by the treatment.

The final irony of the ordeal is the fact that it is Alex's favourite composer's music that is used to accompany the images. It is yet another electronic version of Beethoven's 9th symphony which sends Alex over the edge. He says, 'it's not fair that I should feel ill when I hear lovely, lovely, lovely Ludwig Van.' The serum brings on his repugnance at the images but he is most distressed by the 'sin' of using this music to go with them. In order to try to end his ordeal he comes out with a string of homilies about how he now realises that his actions have been wrong and that he is cured. The doctors don't believe a word of it and he is told that he has to wait.

"Enough of words. Actions speak louder than. Action now. Observe all."

When Alex has been 'cured' he is presented to dignitaries in a theatre at the Ludovico Centre. This scene was shot in South Norwood.

Alex stands in the middle of the stage whilst a spotlight is pointed at him. This reminds us of the underpass and casino scenes as well as the doctors at the Ludovico Centre whose heads are lit from behind. For much of this scene, Alex appears in silhouette as the shots are taken from the back of the stage with the light pointing towards us. He has to shade his eyes and therefore becomes the object of the gaze of the audience without himself being able to see them clearly. This is very much like another interrogation scene. We also see a couple of shots from his point of view when he is told to lick his attacker's shoe and when he looks up to the bare breasts of the woman. The Minister is the master of ceremonies and gives a speech along the lines of a party political broadcast expounding the right-wing virtues of law and order. He confirms his cynicism when he talks about opinion polls to his assistant. His only concern seems to be his own re-election. At he end of his speech, his use of language changes. Up until this point, he has been orating in the manner of a lecturer but now he discards proper sentences and uses clichés to introduce the show.

The chief officer from the prison also appears in this scene as a member of the audience. Although he doesn't say anything, his reactions to what is going on are interesting. During the Minister's first speech when he is talking about the failure of the prison system, the chief officer looks uncomfortable and at one point averts his eyes. His arms remain folded throughout and he even refuses to applaud with everyone else. He smiles when Alex is forced to lick the sole of his attacker's shoe and sits open-mouthed at the sight of the semi-naked woman. This vision does induce him to applaud and as the woman leaves the stage, we see him grinning as he claps energetically. When the Minister is explaining what has just happened, the chief officer looks completely bemused at his use of language and furrows his brow. This character's attributes have just been shown to us without him having to utter a word. His pride is hurt but these feelings disappear when he sees Alex suffering. He is a classic prude as was shown in prison chapel but he is stimulated by what we assume is an unusual sight for him. The stimulation that he feels does not extend to his intellect, as he cannot grasp the fairly simple concept that is being explained. He represents the old way of penal reform and we have just witnessed the new version.

The two performers who take part in the show are also worthy of mention. The man does not, at first sight appear to present much of physical threat to Alex and indeed his initial performance is fairly camp. This is the whole point. Previously, Alex's reaction to being slapped in the face would have been swift and decisive. This man is chosen to show how feeble and defenceless Alex has become. The woman, on the other hand, reminds us of the figures in the Milkbar with her stylised wig and underwear. Both she and the man enter the stage dramatically and leave in the manner of stage performers receiving their applause. This emphasises the unreality of the situation which has been set up to prove a point, whilst at the same time contrasting it with the actual pain and suffering that Alex undergoes.

Each of the tableaux has its own musical accompaniment. The man performs to the strains of 'Overture to the Sun' by Terry Tucker. The music suggests medieval theatre in which cruelty and bloodletting forms part of the entertainment. The woman enters to the film's opening title music that alerts us to the menace to come and Alex stares at her as he raises himself from the floor. She walks slowly towards him with a blank look on her face and the almost full length shot of her body contracts to a head and shoulders shot. Eventually her breasts fill the screen and at his point we see the chief officer's open-mouthed gaze. When she has reached him, she looks down at Alex for the first time and we see her gaze from his point of view. The frame contains her face and breasts and then we see his hands appear from the bottom of the screen as he attempts to touch her. We cut to the opposite shot from her point of view, looking down at him and at this point the nausea comes over him and he collapses once again on the floor. As she leaves the stage, she makes a great show of acknowledging the audience's applause and even pirouettes as she walks off. The man has made similar gestures on his exit but he also waves his left arm in the direction of Alex, in a sense asking that some of the audiences praise should be directed at him for having played his part in the performance. This whole scene is a show and the theatricality of it reinforces the idea that most of the people involved, including Alex, are putting on a performance. This point is further reinforced when Alex recovers his composure and asks the minister, 'was it all right sir, did I do well sir?', as if looking for affirmation of his acting. We know the physical distress that he feels is real but there is still a nagging doubt as to his general sincerity. The prison chaplain enters the scene and restates his doubt about the treatment. It is interesting to note that we cut from the long shot of the group by the stage to the close-up of Alex as the chaplain says the word 'insincerity'. Alex, at first, looks at him with mild confusion that echoes the chief guard's. As the minister speaks, however, he turns to him and smiles as he makes another speech about law and order. Alex reacts to him and to the applause of the audience with a self-satisfied grin. He has no further use of the chaplain. The cuffs of the Minister's shirt are also quite interesting. They are made up of small black and white checks that are very reminiscent of the details of police uniforms.

"I'm completely reformed"

As Alex returns home, we are reminded of the decor of his parents' flat. The hallway has two pictures of semi-naked women on the walls but they are not of the type that we have seen in Alex's room or in those of his victim's. These are examples of mass produced art and the contrast with Alex's taste could not be more striking. The music that is playing on the radio as he walks in is the antithesis of what we have heard so far. It is a jolly ditty about marriage and home life and seems to be pointing up the disparity between Alex's view of life and that of his parents'. One of the first things that he sees is his old bedroom. He expects to find it as he left it but is surprised to see that all of his personality has been removed from it along with his possessions. Not only that but the door is wide open. At first glance, the interior of the room resembles two things. Firstly it looks much more like the rest of the flat with its floral curtains, in place of the Beethoven blind, and pink valances. It is untidy but it reminds much more of what a typical young man's room would look like than Alex's decor did. His large mirror and wall lamp have gone and with the addition of photographs plastered over the wall, it has become reminiscent of his prison cell. This is just the kind of environment that he has been trying to escape from throughout the film.

Before he gets to the living room where his parents are, we see three different newspapers, the headlines of which tell of Alex's release. The first one we see is the Daily Mirror that simply states, 'CAT-WOMAN KILLER ALEX FREED'. The second, the Daily Telegraph says, "CRIME CURE' WILL STRENGTHEN LAW & ORDER POLICY'. Lastly we see the Daily Mail the headline of which is, 'Murderer freed: 'Science has cure". This range of the British press broadly represents the three main classes of society, namely working, upper and middle. It would only have required one of the papers to be shown if the function was to inform us that his parents are now aware of his release. The intention seems to be to make a number of points in as short a space of time as possible. Firstly we see how the case has become a national story and that it is of interest to all strata of society. We also note the differences in the newspapers' use of language. The Daily Mirror refers to Alex as a 'Killer', whereas the other papers do not mention him at all. The Daily Telegraph talks about law and order that are subjects close to the heart of a paper that has traditionally been seen as fairly right wing. The Daily Mail concentrates on the more specific term 'murderer' but puts the claim that the problem is solvable in quotation marks. The final reason for the range and number of newspapers is twofold. It is not unreasonable to expect that if one's son had been the subject of a national news story that one might buy various editions in order to see how the story is reported. It also allows us to be introduced to Joe. From what we learn subsequently, Joe has become part of the family while Alex has been away and we have seen that somebody has taken over what Alex sees as his rightful place in the form of his bedroom. Now we see this, as yet unnamed, character literally 'at home' with Alex's parents. This is shown by his actions which mirror theirs'. He sits on the sofa, eating and drinking and reading a newspaper in the same way that they do. Later on, when he stands up, his clothes blend in with the wall of the living room whereas Alex's dark suit stands out against the softer tones of his parents' attire.

As the situation becomes clear to Alex, the sorrowful music that we heard at the beginning of the prison sequence recurs. Joe tells him that he doesn't believe that he is cured and that he deserves to suffer for what he has put his parents through. Our feelings of sympathy for Alex are brought back by the use of the sombre music that carries on into the next scene.

"Can you spare some cutter me brother?"

Alex is then seen walking east along Chelsea Embankment towards Albert Bridge. He stops and stares at the bridge while he ponders his fate. The bridge itself is almost exactly the same now as it was at the time but with the addition of central support that was added to strengthen it in the 1970's. The Embankment and even the view behind Alex looking along the river towards Battersea Bridge have hardly changed at all. Whilst looking across the river, he is approached by the tramp that we first saw at the beginning of the film in the underpass. The tramp initially asks for money, using the same words as in the earlier scene, but soon turns violent when he realises who it is that he is talking to. He drags Alex, who cannot resist, into another underpass that runs under the bridge and remains almost entirely unchanged to this day. There he is set upon by other tramps but is finally 'saved' by two policemen who turn out to be Dim and Georgie.

As he stares into the River Thames, he appears to be contemplating suicide. A number of elements contribute to this impression. The funereal music and Alex's facial expression as he looks at the water combined with the slow zoom in to the eddies below the bridge leave us with a strong feeling of doom. He looks up at the bridge and then down in to the river as if he is rehearsing his fall. There is also an interesting absence here. Up until this point we have become used to Alex telling us how he feels at moments of high emotion. The visual codes are so strong at this point that his voice-over has become redundant. The arrival of the tramp brings him up short and the two eventually recognise each other. Alex is dragged into the underpass and the scene becomes a mirror of the earlier one in which the tramp is beaten up by Alex and his gang. This time the roles are reversed and Alex makes the point that, 'it was old age having a go at youth'. He also refers to himself again as, 'your humble narrator', and we are about to be asked to identify with his plight once more. The fact that Georgie and Dim are now policemen reminds us of a kind frying pan and fire situation. They have saved him from a beating but we know that they are unlikely to leave it at that. And so it proves. It is also worth noting Alex's shock at finding his previously criminal friends in a position of authority. At the end of the film he is offered the same deal when the minister asks him to work for the government. A strong political point is being made here about the nature of power and violence. The authorities are trying to deal with the problem of violence but also with political dissent. They are quite prepared to turn a blind eye to the former if it can be channelled, for their purposes, into the suppression of the latter.

The numbers on the lapels of Dim and Georgie are noteworthy. Dim has the number 665 and Georgie has 667. Alex is placed in-between them so his number would be…?

As Alex sees Dim, the music changes to the title music and again continues into the following scene. Alex is now frog-marched into a secluded area where he is beaten and almost drowned by his former followers.

"It was a very good way"

We initially see the group from the front as the two policemen hold onto Alex's arms. The rest of the walk into the woods is shot from behind. This plus the fact that it is shot with a wide-angle lens places us in the scene but also produces the often seen disorientating effect. We are following the walk and become part of the action. We could even be the third policeman of the group. We are about to see an unbridled attack on Alex and this, even allowing for our identification with him, could be seen as a manifestation of our own desire for retribution. As he is led forward, Alex appeals to Dim but finds that his previous control has disappeared. His former Droog is now in the position of power and is about to exercise it. As the walk concludes, we cut to the shot of the water trough where Alex is about to be half-drowned and beaten. The music continues but is now punctuated with electronic sound effects that synchronise with the blows of Georgie's truncheon. This heightens the shock and ferocity of the beating that becomes even more uncomfortable to watch as the second shot continues, unedited, with Alex's head under water for nearly a complete minute. When he is eventually released, against Dim's wishes as 'he's still kicking', the former droogs abandon him to recover.

The lightning that punctuates the transition to the next scene reminds us of an old horror film and sets up the following action. Alex is about to find himself in an even worse nightmare than the one that he has just undergone.

"Home, home, home"

He approaches the writer's house in the rain and crawls towards the door in a similar but more desperate way to that used when he and his gang were last here. His voice-over tells us that he wants to be at home and for a moment our sympathies are aroused, as we understand how desolate and wretched he must be feeling. The feelings of sympathy are quickly dashed, as he turns conspiratorial with us.

The following scene begins in almost exactly the same way as the last time we were in this house. We see the writer typing at his desk and then the doorbell rings. He utters the same words and the camera begins its sideways track. This time, however, the camera movement does not reveal his wife but a bodybuilder, working out. We notice that the writer is in a wheelchair and these changes will soon be explained when he tells Alex of the consequences of his previous actions.

The movement of the bodybuilder through the space and then to the front door also mirrors that of the writer's wife in the earlier scene. As we shall see again and again in this scene, there are not only physical mirrors throughout it, but it constantly seems to be reflecting the events and emotions of Alex's previous visit. In place of the sculpture in which the writer's wife was sitting, a large mirror hangs on the wall. This is our first, strong, hint that the examples of repetition that we have already noticed are significant and worthy of our attention.

Julian, the bodybuilder, has no hesitation in opening the door and in fact Alex is now in the very state that he said his friend was in order to gain access to the house on the night of the attack. Our apprehension that he will be recognised is dispelled as Alex tells us that he is not worried because he was wearing a mask the last time he was here. He didn't wear one when he and his gang beat up the tramp and this omission eventually led to his downfall. In a moment he will metaphorically remove another mask and so complete his undoing. His rendition of 'Singin' in the Rain' removes all pretence that he is an innocent victim and shows a complete lack of judgement on his part. His initial self-confidence makes him lower his guard.

Before he commits this act of folly, the writer gives Alex and us a jolt. He says, 'I know you'. Our hearts beat quicker but what he means is that he has read about Alex in the newspapers. We have seen a number of copies lying on his desk at the beginning of the scene. Why such an intelligent man has not already made the connection between the killer of the Cat lady and his own ordeal is a mystery but it does allow for the full horror of his eventual realisation to be shown later. For the moment, he is extremely excited at the prospect of having this victim of police brutality in his house because he is involved in a group opposed to the government. His excitement is expressed in manic facial and eye movements which again mirror those he exhibited when forced to watch the assault on his wife. He has to control his hands by pressing them together and his face contorts in an exhibition of sexual ecstasy. The final point to make about this part of the scene is to do with the way that he refers to Alex. He calls him, 'my boy', in exactly the same way that the Minister did. Neither of these men see Alex as a human being but merely as a tool to further their own ends.

The writer's phone call reveals his plans for Alex. It also tells us that although he and his conspirators are opposed to the draconian methods of the government's law and order policy, they are prepared to control, 'the common people', in the pursuit of, 'freedom'. Our liberal sympathies are questioned, as it seems that both sides of the political argument are as unprincipled as each other.

As Alex continues with his singing, the writer slowly recognises the song and realises that he has given shelter to his wife's murderer. His utter horror is shown very simply. His face contorts and his mouth gapes wide open. This is how we saw him as his wife was being attacked. He shot from below with a wide-angle lens that adds to the distortion of his features and also allows us to see his hands as they grip his trousers. Finally, Alex's singing also becomes distorted as it now echoes through the writer's head. Echoes is a very appropriate term as this whole scene has resonated with links and references to the earlier one.

"Try the wine"

We next see Alex, alone, sitting at a dining table, eating a plate of spaghetti. We might have expected him to have been taken away once his identity had been revealed but this scene draws out the agony. We, the audience, know, for the first time, a piece of information that Alex is as yet unaware of. We know that the writer has discovered who he is but, although Alex's suspicions are raised by the change in the attitude of the writer and his bodyguard/companion, he still feels relatively safe.

This scene is full of black humour. We are acutely aware of the impending doom that awaits Alex even though we don't know what form it will take. This is initially signalled by the aforementioned change in the writer's attitude and the comedy comes in the form of his barked questions to Alex. They make both Alex and us jolt but also break some of the tension that we are feeling. Visually, we are given clues to the new situation. The writer and Julian, the bodybuilder, sit on each side of Alex like guards. Julian sits with his arms folded and both of them stare at Alex while he is eating. Another striking point is that Alex is now dressed in the same dressing gown that the writer was wearing on the night of the attack. We know what happened to the writer and our sense of foreboding for Alex is therefore intensified.

We have all seen incidents in films in which one person has tried to drug another with a spiked drink and when the writer pours Alex a glass of wine, we know what to expect. In most other films the person trying to administer the drug attempts not to draw attention to the fact. Here, however, the writer either doesn't have the subtlety, can't be bothered or is merely relying on Julian's presence. Either way, neither Alex nor we are left in any doubt that drinking the wine is not going to be beneficial to his health. The writer continues to stare intently at Alex and the glass that all but gives the game away. Alex tries to avoid drinking the wine for as long as possible but eventually succumbs to the inevitable. He feigns a knowledge of fine wine but when he does take a drink, he swallows the whole glass in one.

The words 'my wife' again bring Alex up short as he fears the discovery that we know has already been made. The writer rants on about what became of his wife but his demeanour changes slightly as he appears to sympathise with Alex's lot. As the doorbell rings and Julian goes to answer it, Alex tries to make his excuses. Julian turns as Alex stands up and the idea that he is trapped is reinforced. When Julian returns with the conspirators, the atmosphere changes to a pleasant and easy going one. The two new members of the group appear, on the surface, to be sympathetic and eager to help Alex. Their disdain for him, however, is barely disguised as we can see by the way that they talk to him and smirk amongst themselves. They ask him about the police attack but seem to find it amusing more than anything else.

Alex is now surrounded and his deferential demeanour is heightened as he continues to refer to the others as 'sir' and 'missus'. He believes them when they tell him that they want to know the details of what has happened to him and the effects that this has had on him. He is very concerned that they get his exact words and even looks at the pad on which they are being written. He doesn't realise that all they are interested in is information that they can use for their own ends. The way that he describes that he is feeling is very close to the condition that the writer's wife was left in after the attack and which contributed to her death. At this point, we cut to a close up shot of the writer's face as he stares fiercely at Alex. As the drug takes effect and he collapses, face down, into his food, the writer lifts his head and exhibits the same manic stare, in a close up shot that we have seen throughout this scene.

"Turn it off"

When his identity, as the leader of the gang of attackers at the beginning of the film, is revealed to the conspirators, he is taken to another house where he is tortured with the help of Ludwig Van Beethoven. This scene was shot in what was then a country club on

Barnet Lane Elstree that has now become the Edwarebury Hotel.

This scene takes place in two parts of the same house. Alex is locked in an upstairs room that is starkly decorated in mainly white. It is a very bright room and contrasts with the dark and sombre tones of the room below. In this second room we initially see the writer staring up at the ceiling, his face contorting in time to the music that is blasting out. Alex has already told us that it is Ludwig Van and we can see that he is now being tortured on the basis of information that he has revealed to the conspirators. As they hear his cries of pain, they, with the exception of the writer, stand impassively. The chief conspirator rolls balls across a snooker table and watches as they disappear into one of the pockets. They are playing with Alex and have to be patient while he takes his turn. He doesn't take long to decide what his move should be and once the decision is made, he quickly acts upon it.

Both parts of the scene start with a zoom out to reveal the setting and both shots begin on the face of the main characters. Alex and Mr Alexander (the writer) are mirror images of each other. In some ways they are as different as chalk and cheese but in others they exhibit very similar characteristics. Apart from their names there are the opposite attitudes to life and role reversal. Alex works on instinct, expresses himself and gets his pleasure physically. Mr Alexander writes and lives in a solitary world of intellectual activity. Their habitats are very similar to each other as mentioned before being characterised by large expanses of white punctuated by areas of strong colour. When it comes to torture, even the enlightened Mr Alexander can gain as much pleasure as Alex from causing pain.

Alex's pain, as exhibited by his stare, causes him to attempt suicide. We see him climb onto the windowsill and plunge down to the ground below. The point of view shot as we, the audience, fall with Alex was achieved by throwing a camera out of the window.

"I did not snuff it. If I had snuffed it I would not be here to tell what I told have"

His final 'rehabilitation' takes place in a hospital that is north of London.

When we see Alex next, he has returned, visually, to his former state. We have not seen him in his Droog uniform since the police interrogation room but his head-to-toe plaster cast makes for a striking reminder of his prior garb. Everything else that he has worn throughout the film has been fairly dark.

Alex's breathing gives way to moaning which is echoed by a nurse in the throes of ecstasy behind a hospital curtain. We know that Alex experiences a great deal of pleasure through violence and here we see both acts paralleled. Alex's violent injuries and the pain that he suffers are mirrored by the nurse and doctor's sexual act. As they emerge from behind the curtain, their state of undress is necessary to reinforce the idea that Alex's is the only patient in this ward and that we were hearing what we thought we were hearing. Their presence also allows them to discover that Alex has woken from his coma. We know this as he has already told us so and as he says, 'if I had snuffed it, I would not be here to tell what I told have'. This is the end of the story. We are about to reach our conclusion. Alex has been our narrator for the past two hours and we have followed his ups and downs hopefully with great interest. We have been appalled by his acts of violence and found his 'genuine desire to reform' laughable but somewhere inside there lingers a desire to know what will become of him. We are concerned for his future. We must pay close attention to the next fifteen minutes if we want to come away from this film with any sense of closure. The three main conversations that take place are full of revealing sections. When his parents come to visit, we see that they are followers of fashion in more senses than one and also that Alex bears grudges. The examination by the female doctor shows that Alex has regained some of his former appetites as well as disclosing that something happened to him whilst he was in the coma. The main section involves the Minister and his 'speech' is worth paying attention to.

Before we see Alex fully awake, we are treated to some more newspaper headlines. The contrast between these and the earlier examples is noteworthy. This time, Alex is seen as a victim and the government is blamed for not only his condition but also his attempted suicide. The attitude of the newspapers has completely changed and Alex is no longer a killer but is referred to by one of them as a 'boy'. He has become blameless, like a child. The newspapers, of course, contain no sense of irony at the fact that they are now standing up for Alex.

As the headlines end we see Alex lying on his hospital bed being watched over by his P and M. He immediately asks them 'what makes (them) think (they) are welcome', which starts his mother crying. She

doesn't say a word, as was the case when Alex
returned home in the earlier scene, but merely sobs
while Dad tries to placate their son. She wears a bright
red plastic coat that appears to be inappropriate for
someone of her age and Dad's words show that they
are both easily swayed by prevailing fashions, be they
sartorial or political. Alex remains silent and lets Dad
tell us that the whole world has changed its attitude
towards him. Even the fruit basket that they have
brought him is wrapped in plastic like his mother and
this shows a conventional and unsuitable aspect. Alex is
in no condition to enjoy the fruit and his parents have
dressed up because that is what you are supposed to
do when visiting someone in hospital.

"Do you know anything about dreams?"

As the doctor pushes her trolley towards us, she is
placed in a long reverse tracking shot that consequently
gives the shot the deep-space-perspective that we have
seen before. The idea that Alex is alone is reinforced
here as we can see that there are no other patients and
only one nurse and a guard at some distance. The
doctor is wearing the standard white coat but it is
contrasted by her orange dress and purple hair. These
elements take us back to Alex's former environment
where strong colours were used but in the context of a
white setting. When she introduces herself as a
psychiatrist we hear that she has a very mannered way
of speaking in the same way that Mr Deltoid did in
earlier scenes. Alex makes fun of her but she doesn't
react. He asks her about his dreams and as he
describes what he imagined happening to him while he
was in his coma, she looks shocked as if a terrible

secret has been revealed. She covers her shock by responding as if reading from a textbook and quickly getting on with her slide show. It appears that the doctors in this hospital have been trying to reverse the effects of the Ludovico Treatment and that her job is to test the effectiveness of this 'playing around'. Alex is not supposed to be aware of this process.

The slides themselves assess Alex's reactions to various situations. He shows by his responses that he has regained his humour, violent attitude and no longer feels revolted by sex. We might expect the doctor to again be shocked but she seems to be extremely pleased with Alex. He asks how many he got right and she says that it isn't that kind of test but it does appear to be exactly that kind of test and Alex has passed with flying colours. In order to back up the idea that Alex's responses were exactly what were required, she says that he seems, 'well on the way to making a complete recovery'.

"What job and how much?"

Alex's visit from the Minister starts with a shot of him being fed by a nurse. As the Minister arrives, we observe the scene from Alex's point of view, his feet appearing at the bottom of the shot. The first couple of lines are spoken directly at us. The Minister apologises to the doctor for arriving during Alex's meal but the doctor tells him that it is, 'no trouble at all'. Alex's thoughts on having a meal that he is clearly enjoying interrupted are not considered important. The Minister calls Alex, 'my boy' again and seems unconcerned that he is lonely and in pain. His only reason for helping Alex with his food appears to be embarrassment at the mess that he is making of trying to feed himself. He apologises for what has happened to Alex but blames others like the good politician that he is. He also admits that the treatment has been reversed when he says, 'we put you right'. We notice the irony of the statement that, 'there are certain people who wanted to use you for political ends'. We know that this is exactly how he and the government have tried to manipulate Alex but he still sees his motives as completely different from those of the conspirators.

Throughout the rest of the scene, The Minster continues to feed Alex while telling him that he is now safe from the writer and his friends. The act of feeding someone else is a very subordinate one but Alex is relying on the Minister for sustenance in the same way that the Minister needs Alex to sustain him in his position of power. He persuades Alex that if he helps the government, he will get, 'a good job on a good salary'. In response to Alex's question, the Minister does not specify what this will be but we can assume that it will involve the manipulation of public opinion either by political or violent means.

Alex listens as a child would to its father and seems to be most concerned with the food. He oversteps the mark when he asks the Minister what his name is. The Minister coughs but allows Alex to become over familiar with him. Alex is too important to his plans and he does not allow himself to become offended. As a precursor to this he, for the first time, refers to Alex by his first name.

At the point that the Minister asks whether he is making himself clear, Alex starts to pay attention and repeats a line from earlier in the film. He says, 'as an unmuddied lake Fred, as clear as an azure sky of deepest summer, you can rely on me Fred'. These are the exact words that he spoke to Mr Deltoid in his parent's bedroom. He was lying then as we suspected but now we may take his words more at face value. Before, he had nothing to gain, apart from a life of conformity, from following the advice of others. Now that he has been through the mill, he will conform to the expectations of those in authority. Fred is so impressed that he beams as he calls Alex a, 'good boy'.

"I was cured all right"

As the scene ends, the Minister reinforces their new relationship and calls them, 'two friends'.

A stereo and speakers that are even bigger than those used to torture him are trundled in, followed by flowers and a host of photographers. Again, they look directly at us while they take our picture and Ludwig Van blasts out from the music system that looks uncannily like the one that was confiscated from Alex's room. The shot is taken using a wide-angle lens with its disorientating side effects. Alex and the Minister continue to pose for the photographers and as the flashes light up his face, Alex enters a trance like state. If we didn't know any better, we might assume he was an epileptic having a fit but we know what's going on inside his head. One of his, 'such lovely pictures', is now shown to us. He writhes, naked in the snow with a woman in an avenue of wedding guests, all shot in slow motion. As the Ludwig Van fades, he says the immortal line, 'I was cured all right'. Immediately, the strains of Gene Kelly's 'Singin' in the Rain' are heard and the end credits appear. His vision of a wedding debased by public sex and the three aural elements that merge into one another show us as clearly as possible that his duplicity remains as strong as ever and that we should be very wary if we ever meet this young man.